a perfect **bird** guide

A guide to selection, housing, care, nutrition, behavior,

health, breeding and species

Contents

Foreword

Keeping birds is a wonderful hobby which has thousands of fans. Birds draw our attention by their ability to fly, their colors, their beautiful songs and their exuberant behavior. It is quite easy to understand why birds attract so many people.

There is a wide range of variety in birds: Fowl, birds of prey, wildlife birds parrots, parakeets, finches and so on. This book is specifically aimed at bird enthusiasts who keep parrots, parakeets or finches in an aviary or an indoor cage, or those who are considering doing so. An experienced enthusiast will also find many useful tips here. All aspects of keeping these birds are covered here, including caging, buying, advantages and disadvantages of the different species, care, health and breeding. The species described in this book include some that are most commonly kept and that are also suitable for beginners, but also a number of bird families that need a bit more attention. To make it short, we have included anything a beginning bird enthusiast needs to know. This book also gives an up-to-date insight into the bird lovers' world with all its different aspects, and we also pay attention to the organized bird breeding sport.

This book is a general bird guide and describes many different species. Due to the variety of species it is not always possible to give specific detailed information accurate for any specie. It is always good to look for additional specific information of the species you want to keep.

Pet express

Black-headed Parrot

PET EXPRESS

A Publication of

Trident Reference Publishing
801 12th Avenue South # 400
Naples, Florida , USA
www.tridentreference.com
T +1 239 649 7077

ISBN 9781600813122
UPC 6-15269-13127-5

If you are thinking about buying one or more birds, it is good to be clear about the consequences in advance.

You are taking on the responsibility for a living creature for some time to come. It is definitely not our intention to talk you out of this idea, as you can have a lot of fun keeping birds. You need to understand what it involves before you get started, however. Keeping a pet means that you need to make sure that your pet gets everything it needs. It cannot go looking for food itself, as it depends on you for this. Do you have anyone to look after your pet when you go on holiday, for example?

If you decide to go ahead and buy some birds, there are several ways you can precede. The first one is to go to a shop or dealer. Here you can find both birds that breeders have given away as excess, as well as several imported species. In the bird scene, almost all birds are ringed with a solid ring. The second possibility is to buy your birds at a bird fair. These are held all over the USA and you can find them announced in bird magazines and on the Internet. At fairs you will encounter dealers, but also enthusiasts who offer their birds for sale. For those of you who are seriously considering breeding birds, the third option is probably the best: to visit some bird breeders. Here you can choose one or more birds. You will also get the chance to see how the birds are caged and what they are fed. Serious breeders also frequently enter competitions and the quality of their birds is therefore often better. The best breeders end up high in the rankings at shows. Bird shows are held all over the

a perfect bird guide

become a member of a bird association or one of the specialist
clubs. Here you will find experts
who can guide you in their respective avicultural field. They will also
be able to advise you when you
buy your breeding pairs.

There are different standards for
many bird species. The standard
describes which requirements a
bird must fulfill to enter bird shows.
If you intend to participate in bird
shows, you should acquaint
yourself with the demands placed
on the birds.
Also inform yourself about the rules
and customs practiced within the
respective association and at
shows. Visit information evenings

and try to get to know some
experienced breeders who could
help you.

Here's a good piece of advice for
beginning bird breeders: do not
spend too much money when
buying your first birds. Start with
some simple but healthy birds and
try to breed some young to gain
experience. If you are sure that the
species you have chosen is the
right one for you, you can try to buy
some better birds at a good breeder's, for example. Be aware that
top birds are often only for sale for
top money. This is a question of
supply and demand, as everyone
wants to buy their birds from a
champion.

Red-and-green Macaw

Most birds live primarily on plant food and especially on (grass) seeds. During the breeding season they gather as many fresh and unripe seeds as possible for their young.

These contain a lot of vitamins and nutrients which are important for the young birds. They are also more easily digestible than the hard dry seeds. In the breeding season, some species add insects and/or larvae to their menu. There are also species that only eat insects or fruit.

Feeding in the aviary

Most enthusiasts, no matter whether they keep their birds as pets or for breeding, feed them ready-made (commercial) seed mixes.
These mixes contain different sorts of seeds and there are different mixes for different species. The complete mixes are sold in pet shops in different sizes. The bigger the package, the more economical it is. If you only keep one bird at home a 1 kg package will last you several weeks. Breeders with dozens of breeding pairs will buy their food in bulk loads of 25 kg. Some breeders mix their own feeds and buy the different seeds separately. It is not worth the effort for just a pet bird or a couple of breeding pairs, and a ready-made seed mix from the shop will be sufficient.

Besides seed mix, your birds will need some more things to stay healthy, such as:

Egg food

All pet shops sell different brands of egg food. It is a necessary complementary food to the seed

Feeding

mixes, because it contains a number of important vitamins and minerals. During the breeding season your birds should be fed egg food every day. The young can digest this much more easily than hard seeds. During the molting season your birds also need these nutrients every day to be able to renew their plumage.

In the rest period, which is the time between the molting and the breeding period, it is sufficient to feed your birds' egg food two or three times a week. You should increase the number of times you feed egg food towards the breeding season in order to get your birds into good breeding condition. Laying eggs and raising young demands a lot from your birds.

Green food and fruit

You can try around to find out what your birds like best. Some birds like to eat something green, such as lettuce, endives, a piece of apple, some carrot, etc. Make sure that you wash everything properly. Never give your birds too much at once, but only feed them small portions which they can eat in a short time. Green food contains a lot of water and not very many nutrients. It is more useful for keeping your birds occupied and to give them something other than seeds once in a while. Too much food with high water content can lead to intestinal problems. Therefore remove any green food that hasn't been eaten from the cage soon, as it goes off quickly (mould can develop).

Grass and weed seeds

You can also try to entice your birds with grass and weed seeds. You can always just pick grass and weeds from your garden, your birds will certainly like them. You will also find chickweed in almost any garden: a small green plant with very small white flowers. The stalks contain a white milky fluid. You can hang up a large bundle of grass and weed seeds in your aviary, and you will find that your birds will enjoy them and be occupied for quite a while. Be very careful where you pick weeds and grass. Never pick them next to a busy road because of exhaust fumes, and also not from ground that has recently been treated with pesticides.

Millet

The millet that you can buy on stems is a little softer than that in seed mixes. It is therefore ideal

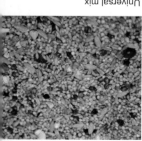

Universal mix

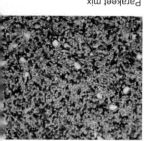

Parakeet mix

Parrot mix

Super worms
Zophobas morio

Buffalo worms

Millet

Stomach gravel

to help young birds learn to eat by themselves. The birds also have a lot of fun eating millet from the stems.

Supplements

Besides the above feeds, your birds also need a number of supplements:

Calcium

Grit (finely ground shells) ensures that the birds get enough calcium. They have to be offered this every day. You can buy grit separately, but it is usually con-tained in the shell sand you use as a floor covering. Another way of pro-viding calcium is to offer your birds the carapace of the squid (sepia). You can buy sepia in any pet shop. You can also grind egg-shells and feed them to your birds. It is advisable to heat these (boil them in water) to kill off any bacteria or germs.

Stomach gravel

These are very fine stones that the birds ingest. They stay within the gizzard and help to grind down the seeds.

Iodine blocks

These blocks contain a lot of mine-rals, such as iodine which prevents problems of the thyroid gland. The blocks also give your birds a good opportunity to gnaw, which keeps the beak in good shape.

Vitamins and minerals

Whole books have been written about these. They are vital for any living creature and ailments develop if there is a lack of vitamins and minerals. Overdosing can also cause problems, however. It will not do any harm to give your birds a course of vitamins at the begin-ning of the breeding season. Make sure you feed them a product which is adjusted to the needs of birds and which contains all the vitamins and minerals in the right proportions. Your birds will normally receive all the vitamins and minerals they need from a balanced diet and giving them extra vitamins is not normally necessary. A sufficient and well balanced diet is better than a medical closet with all sorts of vitamins and solutions.

Water

Every living being consists of water to a large percentage. It is therefore essential that your birds have access to clean drinking water every day. It depends on the species how much water it needs. Birds originating from the rain forest will drink more than birds from savannah areas. The latter

almost always have a split tongue, which allows them to suck up drops of morning dew. Other species have a flat tongue and need to drink more.

However much a bird drinks per day, it is still necessary to rinse the water bottle and fill it with clean water every day. Drinking water becomes soiled very quickly, and mould and bacteria grow particularly quickly in warm weather. They can make your bird seriously ill. Under the influence of light, algae might also grow in the water bottle. The transparent part of the bottle will slowly turn green or brown. Algae are slimy and they allow bacteria to develop. You can buy darker colored drinking bottles in pet shops, in which algae do not grow as quickly.

You can easily clean drinking bottles with a bottlebrush or by putting them in a chlorine solution for a few hours. Make sure that you rinse them well afterwards.

Daily care

To summaries it briefly, daily care consists of refreshing the drinking water and feeding seeds and/or egg food. Take into consideration that drinking bottles can also leak once in a while.
You need to check the seed container every day. It sometimes appears to be still full, whereas it is actually only covered in husks. The birds peel the seeds and leave the empty husks behind. You can blow the empty husks out of the

container and then you will see how many seeds remain. If you are going on holiday you need to make your bird sitter aware of this. It would not be the first time that birds starved to death while it looked as if their feed bowl was still full. I think that every pet shop has clients in during the holiday period who are looking for a bird that looks exactly like the poor thing that starved to death in the short time that they were supposed to look after it.

Remove any uneaten egg food and possibly green food from the cage every day to prevent bacteria growth.

Most bird species can be kept in the living room without too many problems. There are many different types of cages, which you can buy in pet shops. With some DIY skills you can also make a suitable cage yourself.

In the living room
If you don't want to find feathers, sand and empty husks on the floor, then you should keep your birds outdoors. Birds are messy. This is unavoidable, but you can collect the mess under or in front of the cage so that it is not spread throughout the house. Birds also excrete a certain substance through their feathers, which some people are allergic to.

The size of the cage or indoor aviary depends on the kind en on the

number of birds you want to keep. Make sure that the birds have enough space for flying. A narrow high cage is less suitable than a longer one, as birds usually fly horizontally and hardly ever vertically. Also, don't clutter the cage with too many toys which would decrease the flying space. A cage should be at least 20 inches long for one or two birds the size of canaries.

Where to put the cage
Place the cage for your birds on a well-lit place in your living room. Never put it in front of a window where the birds would be exposed to sunlight all day. Birds do enjoy sitting in the sun, but they must be able to decide when they'd rather be in the shade.

The best place for a cage is against a wall. Birds also feel safer here, as people can only walk

Caging

along the cage on one side. If the cage is standing or hanging in a position where people can walk around it on different sides, the birds cannot withdraw and feel less secure.

Make sure that your birds are not standing in a draught, as they cannot cope with this. Make sure that the cage is placed steadily on a table, a stand or a console. A cage that hangs from a chain and moves every time the birds do makes its inhabitants feel very insecure. This will make them very shy.

Fitting out a cage

The interior of a bird cage can be quite simple. Make sure that they have plenty of perches which are attached safely. Too many perches decrease the flying space, however. The perches must be thick enough that the birds can clasp them well. It is best to use perches of varying thickness, as these are best for the birds' muscles. Some cages have thin plastic perches delivered as standard. For a few pence you can replace these with wooden perches of 12 to 15 mm thickness from the DIY store. Willow twigs also make good perches.

It is best to cover the floor of a cage with aviary sand. This usually contains grit which the birds can ingest. At present, you can buy a number of different floor coverings which all have their own advantages and disadvantages. Let the shop assistant advice you on this. Some

people will advise you to use old newspapers as floor covering because it can hold a lot of fluid and is easy to replace. A disadvantage of newspapers is, however, the ink which is harmful to animals and humans alike. If you do use newspapers on the floor, then make sure that you offer your birds grit and stomach gravel in a separate bowl.

Make sure that your birds can easily reach their food and drink bowls or bottles. A bird might have some problems finding its food when it

Cockatiel

Red-cheeked Cordonbleu (l), Double-barred Finch (r)

comes into a new cage. So scatter some food on the floor, this will help the bird get used to its new cage.

For a pet bird, some toys can offer distraction in its cage. You can choose from a large variety of mirrors, bells, ladders etc, in pet shops. Remember, however, not to clutter the cage with toys. Tropical birds have fairly little use for toys, it is better to buy them a companion.

Outdoor aviary

If you have enough space in your garden you can build an outdoor aviary. Take any limitations into account. Building regulations vary per community. Find out before starting your aviary whether you need a permit. Also ask your neighbors whether they would mind.

A suitable aviary consists of a flight with a night shelter attached to it. A lot of bird breeders have a

breeding room indoors and one or more outdoor flights where those birds that are not used for breeding can fly. Some bids breed in colonies in the wild, whereas some only brood as pairs. Bigger species often require an aviary to themselves, but smaller species can often be placed in a so-called communal aviary. It is also important to know something about their natural behavior and the background of the birds.

The size and position of the aviary is, of course, determined by the space available. If you can choose, then an aviary facing east or west is ideal. It is inadvisable to let an aviary face south, as it is then standing in the full sun. North is also not a good option, as it gets dark too quickly and is very cold in the winter.

You need to make sure that the aviary is protected against the full sun in the summer and the wind and rain in the colder seasons. Most outdoor aviaries for birds have a roof, even if it is transparent. This keeps the aviary dry and prevents the floor and the perches from being soiled with the faces of wild birds (which can transfer diseases). It also offers some protection against birds of prey and cats etc.

Building materials

You can use a number of materials to build an aviary. Today the frames of outdoor aviaries are often made of square aluminum tubes. You can buy different couplings for them, which means that building an aviary is quite easy for someone with some basic DIY skills. The material is quite expensive but it needs very little maintenance. Wood is a cheaper alternative, but it is less durable.

You can buy the mesh per meter from a roll in larger bird specialist shops or at the ironmonger's. The mesh does not need to be too heavy for birds. The mesh has usually been galvanized to prevent rusting. New mesh usually shines quite a lot, which can be a nuisance. You can cover it with a darker paint that isn't harmful to birds. This allows a better view of the birds but it also keeps the mesh in good condition longer.

Floor

The floor of the outdoor flight must be dry. A wet floor is a breeding ground for bacteria. Plants in the aviary are not advisable for all

Java Sparrow

birds, as canaries, for example, will destroy them within no time. An aviary with plants attracts insects, which is an extra source of food for many species, but it is generally too little to raise young with it in the breeding season. You need to offer the birds some extra live food then. The interior of an outdoor aviary can vary. The more plants you put in your aviary the less you will be

Canary

able to see your birds. They will hide away and stay very shy.

Perches

You can make perches from turned wood which you can buy in varying lengths in the DIY shop. Many enthusiasts build rows of perches neatly placed one under the other. You can also use twigs from trees. A twisted twig or ragged tree trunk is not only decorative but also gives your birds something to do. There need to be plenty of sitting opportunities in the aviary, but flying space is just as important. Take into considerations that birds like to sleep as high up as possible. If there is little space high up, this can lead to fights.

Night shelter

Because of the danger of nightly disturbances in the aviary through birds of prey and cats, it is best if you get your birds used to

Canary

spending the night in their shelter. The night shelter should therefore be a little higher than the flight. It needs to have highly placed perches and a window so that it stays light as long as possible in the evenings. The birds will then look for a safe sleeping place indoors. If this is not working you can lock the birds up in the shelter

Rainbow Lorikeet

at night. The space and number of perches inside determines on the number of birds that you can keep in the aviary.

The night shelter needs to provide access to the aviary by one or more hatches. Make sure that you can open and close these from outside, so that you don't have to enter the aviary every time you want to open or close them. Cover the windows with mesh so that the birds don't fly against them. This mesh also prevents your birds escaping if a window should get broken for some reason. You can also integrate a door between night shelter and flight. A door directly at the flight also has the risk that your birds escape unless you build a sluice around it.

If you want to breed with your birds, then it is advisable to create an extra room in the night shelter as a flight for young birds. Young birds are independent at approximately six weeks and most pairs will then go over to laying their next batch. It happens quite often that the older birds then see the young as rivals and chase after them in an attempt to chase them away. This can even end in the death of some of the youngsters. You can prevent this by taking them out of the aviary in time. After the breeding season they can quite happily be placed together again.

The feed and drink containers are best attached to the inside. You can place them on the ground, but

it is better if they are a little higher. The bowls are then not soiled as easily by the birds and they are also more difficult to reach for vermin, such as mice. If you release new birds into the aviary, do that in the night shelter, so that they can find the food straight away. Introduce new birds as early in the day as possible and not shortly before it gets dark. They then have plenty of time to get used to their new home and to find the food and drink.

Grey Parrot

As you can see we can only provide some general advice on building aviaries here. It is useless to show you all sorts of plans and designs as your personal circumstances determine what your aviary will look like. It is best to go and visit some breeders, as they will usually be able to give you the best advice on building aviaries.

The inhabitants of an aviary
Canary's cohabitate quite easily, even to the degree that a few

males can live together with more hens. Songbirds are best kept in pairs. You can put several species together but make sure that there is always only one pair per species. Songbirds can also be kept together with canaries. Tropical bird species can be kept outdoors as long as you put them in the aviary in the summer so that they have plenty of time to get used to the outdoors before it turns winter. A solid night shelter is then very advisable. This also applies to other finch species, such as Zebra Finches, Society Finches, Java Sparrows, Shafttails, Indian Silverbills and African Silverbills.

The small African finches, such as the Red-cheeked Cordon bleu, the Red-billed Fire Finch etc. can also be kept outdoors without too many problems. Pet shops with a larger assortment sell heated perches, which the birds use very happily

when it is freezing, as their feet are very sensitive to frost. Cockatiels are friendly birds that can be kept single in pairs or even with other small birds. Budgies can be kept in groups too and mostly with other birds too, but sometimes they can get aggressive to smaller birds, so be careful.

Breeding room

If you decided to breed birds for competition or if you want to breed certain color combinations, you need to have cages in which you can place the separate pairs, as you need to be able to pair the birds up as you want to. You will have to pay attention to color, size, relationship, etc. If you let the birds choose their partners in the aviary you might end up with less desirable combinations, which is why you need breeding cages.

A lot of breeders use a spare room or a shed to establish a breeding room. This consists of a number of breeding cages and one or more flights placed against one wall. When furnishing the room you obviously need to take windows and doors into consideration.

Breeding cages

If you are any good at DIY you can quite easily make breeding cages yourself. You can buy sheets of suitable material in all sorts of sizes. The best choice is white plasticized chipboard, as this is easy to work with and also easy to keep clean. Untreated chipboard has the disadvantage that the glue

gives off toxic gases. This is not healthy for your birds. You can also use multiplex, which is also easy to work with, but it needs to be treated with a non-toxic environmentally friendly paint. It is a bit more difficult to keep clean and you need to repaint it once in a while. The advantage is that you can use another color than white, which the birds find more relaxing.

The most common breeding cages are completely solid apart from the front wall, where a front panel is inserted. You can make this yourself from metal or mesh. Most enthusiasts use ready-made front panels as you can buy them in pet shops in different sizes and styles. They have a door and maybe some flaps for plastic food containers. You can also simply put feeding bowls on the floor. The front panels are very suitable for hanging up water dispensers.

If you intend to build your own cages it is best to buy the front panels first and only start to assemble the cages when you have all the right measurements. You can cover the rough edges of the panels with an aluminum or plastic strip, which you can normally buy in the most common widths.

If you are no good at DIY, then you can choose from a number of ready-made cages. Different vendors normally have their stands at big shows and fairs, and you can also find different contact details in the classified sections of bird magazines.

The cages will not be cheap but it is an investment in something you will use for years to come. They are assembled without screws or nails and you can sometimes take them apart yourself. These system cages often have removable partitions. If you remove these partitions you can offer your birds' big flying' cages. You might be lucky enough to get some second-hand cages.

The minimum measurements for breeding cages are 20 inches long,

Budgerigar

16 inches high and 16 inches wide. Bigger is better, especially when the young are there. If the nesting box is attached to the outside of the cage then you can maximize the birds flying space.

The most commonly used floor covering in breeding cages is aviary sand. It is advisable to make a drawer for the sand which you can easily remove and clean. The easiest solution is a metal tray. If you make your cages yourself, you need to take into consideration that sand and bits of seeds will get between the drawer and the walls. If you make the cages so that the

tray fits in perfectly, then you will have problems removing it if a lot of mess gets stuck in the gaps.

Flights

You can make as many flights of as large a size as you have space available.

Once the young birds are independent you can place them in here. They then have more space available to develop further. You can also place breeding birds in flights during the resting season when they need to get into shape for the next breeding season or the exhibition season. If you want to keep male and female birds separately in the resting season you need to have at least two flights.

Heating

Strictly speaking, heating is not actually necessary to get your birds through the winter.

If they have a dry and sheltered night accommodation or if they are kept in a breeding room they can get by without heating.

The cold is less of a problem to them than the dampness so typical to our winters. If you want to breed in the winter, which a lot of breeders do so that they have grown birds available for the showing season, then you should install heating. It doesn't have to reach tropical temperatures, as this is just a waste of electricity, 50 to 60 °F is enough. You then don't have to put on your winter coat every time you're going to feed your birds. Another advantage is that those birds which have been to a show don't have to acclimatize when they come back. Otherwise show birds constantly move from a warm environment to a cold one and vice versa. Constant temperature changes increase the risk of illnesses.

If you do use heating, make sure that the air doesn't become too dry in the aviary. Especially in the incubation period a humidity of 60 to 65% is necessary to let the eggs hatch normally. If the air is too dry, then the membrane around the embryo will harden and the chick will later not be able to free itself from the egg.

Lighting

Plenty of daylight is important, as your birds will slowly waste away in dark rooms and the breeding results will be disappointing. If you are going to build a breeding room, remember to integrate plenty of windows.

It is best to place one or more transparent panels in the roof, as they will ensure plenty of light from above.

You will usually have to rely on neon tubes to reach a sufficient amount of daylight. Time switches will make sure that the lighting is always switched on and off at the same time. This ensures the regularity which is most like the lighting situation in the wild. If you have to switch the lights on and off manually variations will occur in the length of daylight which will throw

Galah

the birds off balance. They will unexpectedly start molting or abandon their nests, for example. It is best to let the light turn on and off at fixed times. The ideal amount of daylight is 12 to 15 hours in 24 hours. To make the changes from darkness to light less abrupt you should use automatic dimmers.

Oxygen

To keep your birds healthy you need to make sure that enough oxygen gets into their home. You can ensure this with the help of ventilation systems and cantilever windows. To keep vermin (mosquitoes) outdoors gauze blinds are usually installed. The gauze can become clogged up by dust, so you need to clean it regularly.

Behavior

The behavior of birds varies from species to species. Some are very social and live in colonies, some live in colonies during the resting period but separate from the group as pairs during brooding, whereas others live solitary lives.

Some species are not aggressive but quite dominant, such as Zebra Finches. They will often be the first on the food bowl and also the first to choose a nesting box. Java Sparrows, Japanese nightingales and weaver species can sometimes disturb the brooding of other species and even steal the young and eggs. When choosing the species for your aviary take this into consideration if your aim is to breed birds.

When young birds are just about independent you can sometimes tame them. This will require a lot of time and patience every day. It is also important to observe the birds every day.

You will get to know the hierarchy in the aviary and you can intervene in time if necessary.

It is obvious that this hobby requires some time. You don't only need time to look after your birds every day, but you also need to get to know your birds, which means that you need to spend approximately fifteen minutes a day observing and enjoying them. You will then know right away if a bird is not well or if something else is wrong. If you don't have this time then you have too many birds or too little time to look after them properly. You should then ask yourself whether it might be better for your birds if you stop this hobby.

Golden-breasted Waxbill

Cockatiel

Before you start breeding birds you need make sure that a number of prerequisites are fulfilled. The birds must be in good condition, fit to breed and at least a year old.

Breeding process

Experienced breeders usually slowly raise the number of light hours and the temperature to prepare the birds for the breeding season, especially when the breeder wants the birds to breed in winter. Use a time clock and a heater. This method resembles natural processes, as in the wild breeding starts when the days lengthen and the temperatures rise.

These are, however, not the only stimuli the birds react to. When spring comes, nature is full of new life. The trees and shrubs are green and insects reappear. This means a better menu. In winter, the natural resting period, birds only find little and very one-sided food. When this changes in spring it puts the birds into brooding mood, even more than just the light and the temperature. Some bird species only start reproducing when they are sure that they will find enough food for their young. In the wild this is usually during or just after the rainy period. Although some breeders feed the same food all year round, the natural method (i.e. that the diet is adjusted to the seasonal offer) is preferable.

Make sure that your birds get enough gravel and calcium in the breeding period. Females need it to lay good eggs.

If you breed in breeding cages, you can separate the males and females during the rest period and pair

a perfect bird guide

Possible problems during breeding

The brooding process doesn't always run as smoothly as described above. Try to keep an eye on your birds to find out what the causes may be. The most common problems are:

Unfertilized eggs

- The birds you paired up don't really get along. If they cannot get used to each other you should separate them.
- The birds are too young. Put them back into the aviary again and try again later, or break the pair up and give them older partners.
- The mating wasn't successful due to loose perches.

Eggs are fertilized but don't hatch

- The air is too dry in the aviary or sometimes the humidity is too high. A hygrometer will tell you the humidity in the birds' accommodation. The ideal humidity is between 55 and 65%.

Eggs are pricked and thus leak

- The parents' nails are too long. Trim them.

Eggs have been laid but the hen doesn't want to incubate

- You can place the eggs with a pair that broods well.
- The male is chasing the female. Note such characteristics in the breeding logbook.

Young are not fed or only badly

- Here, too, it might be an idea to transfer the chicks to another nest with young of approximately the same age. It is also common to transfer chicks to another nest if there are only one or two young. A nest of three to four young usually develops better as the chicks keep each other warm.

Young are attacked

- The father is usually the culprit. Insert a partition in the breeding cage under which the chicks can hide.

them up in the breeding cages later on. If you are going to breed birds in a communal aviary and there are several birds of one species, then it is best to mark the birds with rings so that you can tell later which ones are the parents.

Make sure that the bird accommodation offers an excess of nesting boxes in different styles. Then there will be enough choice to prevent the birds from fighting. Also offer them plenty of nesting material, such as sisal ropes, coconut fiber, hay and moss. You can put the moss in the nests to start with, as it will keep the humidity level constant. You will not need to interfere with the nest building any further, as the birds can do it much better anyway and they also have a lot more time for it.

When the birds come into breeding mood they will start building their nest as soon as they get the opportunity. If they are in good breeding condition, you will find the first egg after a week. Finches and parakeets usually lay four to six eggs. The incubation time can vary per species. Fertilized eggs usually hatch fourteen to twenty days after incubation started. You can recognize a fertilized egg by its color. It will turn darker after a few days of incubation.

You can also buy special test lamps. An unfertilized egg stays more or less transparent, whereas you can see blood vessels and the heart developing in fertilized eggs after a few days.

You should offer your bird's bath water more often during the breeding season. When the young have hatched they may bathe four times a week. You will also need to give your birds some extra food, such as egg food. You need to refresh this at least once a day. You may also want to add live food to your birds' diet, which you can also buy in handy deep-freeze packs. Not all bird species like live food, as it depends on what they eat in the wild. You may only feed germinated seed if it is absolutely free of mould.

Most species can be ringed five to eight days after they hatched. You can order rings from the different bird associations. The ring size varies from species to species. Have a look in bird magazines in which the ring sizes are given or ask the relevant person at your association. It is important to keep a good breeding logbook. In this

you can note the batch, the ring numbers, when the young were born, if the parents are feeding them well and further information. You can then use these notes when selecting the birds with which you want to breed in the following season.

Most birds are independent after six weeks and they can then be separated from their parents. It is best to place them in a separate breeding or show cage for a week before releasing them into the aviary. They can then become independent in peace. Spray millet is quite a good food to help your birds become independent. When releasing the youngsters into an aviary it is best to put some older birds with them. They can function as teachers and show the babies where to find food and water. After the chicks have been taken away the parents will normally start laying the next batch of eggs straight away. Don't let the pairs breed all year long and limit the batches of eggs to two, three at the most. Give your birds a few months of rest after that. They will then not become exhausted, and you will still be able to enjoy your breeding birds the next year.

Young birds often have an adolescent plumage which differs widely from that of their parents. The chicks' plumage has a natural protective color. The youngsters will normally molt at three months old and the adult plumage will then appear. The wing feathers often only molt in the second year.

Breeding logbook

A good breeding logbook is essential to trace the origins and the inheritance of your birds. What should you note? Here's an example with some standard information.

Breeding logbook example

Breeding year:	Date ringed: ....
Cage number:	Date flown out: ....
Species:	Ring nos. young: ....
Data father	Colour young/remarks: ....
Ring no:	**2nd batch**
Colour:	Date mating: ....
Data mother	Date 1st egg: ....
Ring no:	Number eggs: ....
Colour:	Number fertilised: ....
1st batch	Date hatched: ....
Date mating:	Date ringed: ....
Date 1st egg:	Date flown out: ....
Number eggs:	Ring nos. young ....
Number fertilised:	Colour young/remarks: ....
Date hatched:	

You can extend this form however you wish. The important thing is that you note down all the necessary information. You will get to know your birds better this way, and you can then give the buyers of your birds the right lineage. The way in which you keep your breeding logbook can be simple, from a few loose papers in a folder to a computer database. You can buy whole computer programmers for this purpose. You can transfer the details from the breeding cards to another register in which you note each bird's data, such as ring number, lineage, color, show results, etc. To be able to tell the birds apart you need to ring them. You can order bird rings from bird associations.

Shows

Hundreds of bird shows are held throughout the USA, mostly in the autumn. These are competitions in which the results of the breeding season are judged.

Any local association will have a show at some point. The specialist clubs hold their shows on a regional level, but they also organize national shows. The best birds also go to the bigger regional shows and district competitions.

At the very top, there are also the world championships, which are held in a different European country each year, under the wing of the COM (Confederation Ornithologique Mondial). All species of birds are present at such a show: canaries, exotic birds, parrots, etc.

Gouldian Finch

Birds are living creatures which can also become ill. Nursing a bird is not easy, especially not for a beginning enthusiast.

You can easily recognize an ill bird by its behavior: it is less lively, sleeps a lot, raises its feathers, the eyes are dull or watering, and it has sometimes lost so much weight that you can see the sternum sticking out. If you think that your bird is ill, contact the vet as soon as possible.

Try to explain the symptoms as clearly as possible. Look at the eyes, is the bird gasping for air, what do the faces look like, how does it behave, is it eating well, is it sleeping well, is it sitting on its food bowl all day long? If necessary, the vet can examine the faces and prescribe the appropriate medication.

Make sure that your bird cannot catch a cold during the transport and cover the cage well.

Recognizing a sick bird

It is essential that the keeper notices when a bird is sick as soon as possible, so birds must be checked daily. Even when birds don't appear to be in the best of health, too much time is often lost before corrective action is taken; with the result that the birds do not receive the care they need when they need it. Even though a suspect bird may not be showing symptoms, it must be captured and removed because it might well infect other birds, perhaps by way of its droppings.

Timely recognition and corrective action is also important because sick birds eat little or nothing, and most birds are unable to last more than 24 hours without food.

a perfect bird guide

If sickness is suspected, you should observe the bird without the bird being aware of it. This is because, if a bird is aware of its keeper, it will behave differently, and often pull its feathers tightly against its body making it easy to conclude that there is nothing wrong with it. While it appears that nothing is wrong, the moment the keeper is out of sight, the bird will return to its sick posture (closed eyes, fluffed feathers). Fluffed feathers are the best indication that a bird is sick. A bird showing symptoms may already be in an advanced stage of sickness. Generally, a bird that is visibly ill is also seriously ill.

Sick birds should be isolated in a hospital cage to prevent them from infecting others. The accommodation that the sick bird came from should be disinfected immediately. Feeding bowls, drinking fountains, perches and toys should receive special attention. The keeper should keep an eye out for a few days for symptoms appearing in other birds.

Why do sick birds fluff their feathers?

A sick bird's temperature regulation is disrupted. As a result, it will eat less than normal, lose weight and eventually find it difficult to maintain its body temperature. The bird will attempt to retain heat by fluffing its feathers to insulate itself from the surrounding air. At this stage, it is important that the bird receives additional warmth. You can provide

extra warmth by placing the bird in a hospital cage.

Illnesses and ailments

A vet is the best person to diagnose a sick bird, and the vet is more often than not the person who will supply the medicine. Unfortunately very few vets specialize in bird diseases. Animals, unlike humans, can't tell you what is bothering them. Reaching a diagnosis, especially with birds, is not easy. To help you to recognize bird ailments, I have provided a description of some of the most common ones, together with the associated symptoms and treatments. Before you start doctoring for yourself however, make sure that your diagnosis is correct. If you are in any doubt at all, you should consult a vet. The same applies to ailments not mentioned in this book.

Gouldian Finches

Blood mite (red bird mite)

The red bird mite is a very small, barely visible spider-like animal. Blood mites can appear in any birdhouse and reproduce rapidly in warm weather. Red bird mites hide in splits, cracks and holes during the day and emerge at night to suck the birds' blood. Once they have sucked themselves full, mites are recognizable as red dots. The presence of blood mites can be confirmed by wiping a knife blade along cracks and joins in the bird-cage. If blood mites are present, traces of blood will be visible on the blade. Mites do not present an immediate danger for birds, but they will weaken the birds over time.

Treatment: eradicate blood mites with a mite spray. The spray must not be harmful to birds – check the label for information. Blood mite sprays may be bought at pet shops.

Diarrhea

See intestinal infection (enteritis).

Intestinal infection (enteritis)

Diarrhea is one of the specific characteristics of intestinal infection. In addition, birds with an intestinal infection will sit apathetically crumpled up with their heads buried in their feathers, seriously sick. There can be many causes of intestinal infection, such as:

- **Spoiled food**
  Food can become rancid if it is not stored properly. Damp egg food/energy food mix is liable to deteriorate and decay, especially in hot weather. Birdseed must always be stored in dry and cool conditions. Give egg food and strength food as much as possible in a dry state. In warm weather, egg food mix should be replaced twice a day.

Moluccan King-Parrot

Golden Parakeet

- **Too much iron in the food**
  Grayish diarrhea can be caused by water containing a high percentage of iron, perhaps from well water or water from rusty drinking bowls. The solution is to provide tap water or to use other drinking bowls.
- **Excessive fluid retention**
  Causes for this can be food that is too salty and/or the provision of too much green food. Check the ingredients of the food and temporarily stop providing green food.
- **Draughty accommodation**
  Draughts in the cage can stress the birds, which can lead to sickness. The obvious solution is draught-free accommodation.
- **Poisoning**
  Green food treated with insecticide can cause diarrhea. Green food

must always be washed thoroughly before it is given to birds.

Treatment for diarrhea

The first step is to wash any feathers covered in droppings with a sponge and lukewarm water. The sick bird should then be placed in a hospital cage where the temperature should be about 95 °F. To enable the bird to regain energy, provide simple sugars, dextrose for example. Dilute the simple sugars in water before giving them to your bird. The water should not be too cold and it should be replaced twice a day. If the bird is too weak to drink, the sugar solution can be fed directly into the bird's crop with a crop needle. As food, you can provide anti-diarrheal seeds. In addition you can give rusk crumbs mixed with a little charcoal powder.

Regent Parrot

This vomit consists of a sticky slime. By shaking its head to and fro the bird eventually covers its face, head and neck feathers with slimy vomit. A bird suffering from crop disease will die within 24 hours if treatment is not given.

Treatment: The only effective treatment for this disease is to administer an antibiotic. Antibiotics may be obtained from a vet.

Egg-binding

A female unable to lay her eggs is said to be egg-bound. A hen suffering from egg-binding will sit on the floor of the cage with fluffy feathers. Egg-binding often occurs with hens that are very young. Egg-binding can also be caused by large temperature fluctuations or severe cold.

Eye infections

Eye infections may occasionally appear during the winter or in poorly ventilated rooms. In the case of the latter, the ventilation needs to be improved.

Treatment: Treat the affected eye with boracic lotion or boiled water, which is cooled to tepid before you apply it. Rinsing should be done with a water-soaked cotton wool bud. Each cotton wool bud should only be used once.

A stubborn eye infection will need to be treated by a vet.

Ornithosis

Ornithosis is caused by a virus. The symptoms are fluffy feathers, breathlessness, infected eyes and a runny nose. The bird's feathers

After consuming simple sugars, the bird will recover quickly and be able to eat normal food again. As soon as there is an improvement, you can stop giving the simple sugar dissolved in water. The temperature of the hospital cage should then be gradually reduced. It is always sensible to consult a vet.

Overgrown beak

The lower beak sometimes continues growing, especially the beaks of hooked-nosed birds, like Cockatiels. This can make it difficult to eat for the bird.

Treatment: Simply cut the beak with a pair of scissors or nail trimmers.

Crop disease

Birds with crop disease constantly empty the contents of their crop.

are often contaminated with the discharge from the nostrils. This sickness is infectious to both birds and humans.

Treatment: In the event of ornithosis consult a vet, who may prescribe antibiotics.

Leg fractures

Leg fractures can be caused by accidents or fighting. Birds have been known to fracture a leg when startled at night. A small night-light will reduce this risk.

Treatment: A broken leg needs to be immobilized. The leg can be immobilized using a straw that has been cut open lengthways, or a feather shaft. The leg needs to be held straight and bandaged with one or two strips of Elastoplasts. The bird should be housed separately in a cage without perches,

Superb Parrot

and should be fitted with a neck collar to prevent it from pecking at the bandages. The bandages can be removed after fourteen days, by cutting them off carefully.

Knemidokoptic mange (scaly leg and face disease)

Knemidokoptic mange, also called cere mites, or scaly leg and face disease, is rare in Cockatiels in Australia. It is caused by a microscopic mite called Knemidokoptes pilae. These mites live on the birds day and night, and cause large numbers of wart-like growths by tunneling into the skin and feeding on the tissue. The symptoms are often seen first in the beak's wax skin. The disease can be transmitted to other birds.

Treatment: An infected bird should be treated with an anti-parasitic drug such as ivermectin. Infected birds should be referred to a vet.

Feather lice and feather mites

Feather lice and feather mites can inhibit the development of growing feathers and cause feathers to fall out.

Eclectus Parrot

To ensure you have the right diagnosis, take some feathers to the
vet. The feathers should be placed
in a tightly sealed plastic bag
immediately after they have been
plucked. Do not use any feathers
that are lying on the floor of the
cage because they may no longer
carry any lice or mites. Feather lice
and feather mites should be treated
with an insecticide. In the event of
infection by feather lice or feather
mites, always consult a vet.

Injuries

Minor and major injuries can occur
quite easily from fights and accidents. Small wounds heal
spontaneously in most cases.
Larger wounds, especially head
wounds, need to be treated.
Treatment: Injured birds, like all
sick birds, should be segregated to
prevent other birds from pecking
their wounds. Disinfect the wound
with tincture of iodine or another
disinfectant. The wound should be
dressed if necessary and, if possible; the bird should be fitted with a
neck collar to ensure that it doesn't
peck at either the dressing or the
wound. Large wounds should
always be referred to a vet, and
may need stitching.

Wing fractures

Wing fractures are almost always
the result of accidents.
Treatment: If a bird sustains a
wing fracture, the wing should be
strapped to the body with a bandage. The bandage must be
wrapped around the bird three
times. The first wrapping is around
the breast and wing roots. The
second is around the belly and the
middle of the wings, and the third
around the tail and the wing tips.
The bandage may be removed
after about two weeks. You must
be extremely careful not to restrict
the bird's chest movement.

Worms

Cockatiels are only rarely affected
by worms. A worm infection occurs
when a bird comes into contact
with the worm eggs or larvae from
infected birds. In the case of a
chronic infection, a general deterio-
ration in condition and weight loss
will be visible. If nothing is done to
intervene, the bird will eventually
die. Worm infections often occur in
the warm months of summer.
Worms can infect the intestines or
the airways.
Treatment: Birds infected with
worms need to be treated with a
wormer, which must be

Scaly-breasted Munia

administered strictly according to the instructions on the label. A good way to worm a bird is to administer the remedy with the aid of a dropper or crop tube. Because of the danger of infection, the bird-cage or aviary must be thoroughly cleaned while the worming is being carried out and new perches must be fitted. The drink and feeding bowls also need to be cleaned and disinfected. Several treatments may be needed.

Bird euthanasia

Conducting bird euthanasia is one of the most unpleasant things that a bird fancier can experience. Luckily most forms of illness and ailments are preventable but in those cases where a bird won't recover, the keeper must ask himself how much longer does the bird have to suffer, and would it be better to release it from its suffe-ring? Helping an incurable or termi-nally sick bird to die quickly, and above all painlessly, can best be done using ether. Place the sick bird in a plastic bag and pour in a small amount of ether (about 15 ml is more than sufficient). Tie the bag closed. When the bird has died, dispose of the body.

Disinfectants and pesticides

Disinfectants combat sickness and pesticides combat vermin.
A disinfectant is used to cleanse a birdcage of bacteria, viruses and mould. A pesticide is used to com-bat both external parasites, such as lice and mites, and internal parasites, such as worms.

Hyacinth Macaw

Disinfectants

Whenever a bird catches an infec-tious disease, it is necessary to disinfect the complete birdcage, including the drinking and feeding bowls. The sick bird must be cap-tured and isolated without delay, both so you can treat it more effec-tively, and to prevent other birds from becoming infected. It is highly likely that the sick bird has infected not only the birdcage but also the contents, which is why it is essen-tial to disinfect everything thoroughly. Disinfectants need to be chosen with care.
Follow the instructions on the packet closely and replace the perches with new ones.

Pesticides

As already mentioned, pesticides are used to combat vermin.
Feather lice and blood mites are

Canary

cage in a warm spot, for example on a central heating radiator or next to a stove. A thermometer is necessary to check the temperature. The temperature in a hospital cage needs to be about 95 °F. The bird will generally drink more water because of the heat. The correct air temperature for a sick bird can be judged from its behavior. If the bird remains huddled up like a ball then the temperature is possibly still too low. If the bird starts panting with its beak open, then the temperature is too high.

Despite its need for warmth, the bird also needs to be able to move to a cooler spot. You also need to prevent too much light from entering the hospital cage, because too much light can irritate the bird. No matter where you place the cage, the location needs to be quiet and free of draughts and smoke.

examples. Pesticides need to be chosen with care and the instructions printed on the label must be followed carefully.

What are the requirements of a hospital cage?

A hospital cage for most little and medium-sized birds should be about 20 inches high, 20 inches deep and 24 inches wide.
A good hospital cage is fitted with built-in heating, often in the form of an infrared lamp, and a thermometer is fitted on the inside. The warmth of an infrared lamp penetrates a few millimeters into the skin of a sick bird. Make sure that the hospital cage is easy to clean and disinfect.

It is also possible to put a sick bird into a regular cage and place the

Making your own hospital cage

The following points are important when you are constructing a hospital cage. The front of the cage can be fitted either with Perspex or bars. Fit the cage with a large door. Make the cage from material which is easy to clean, such as aluminum.

Fit the cage with a thermometer.

Fit the cage with a heating source, such as an infrared lamp, or place the cage above a central heating radiator or next to a stove. If you use an infrared lamp it is important that the bird has enough space in

a perfect bird guide

the cage to be able to escape from the heat source if it becomes too hot. The risk of overheating will be les of a problem if you use an open cage and place it either on or in front of a radiator.

Fit a sliding tray under the bottom of the cage so that droppings can be easily removed.

Make a gauze mesh screen to floor to help it maintain its balance. The thickness of a perch should be such that the bird is not quite able to close its claws completely around it.

Lay waterproof material, such as plastic or greaseproof paper in the bottom of the sliding tray, so that droppings are easily seen.

Diamond Firetail

cover the sliding tray to prevent the bird from walking in its own droppings. The size of the perforations in the mesh should be suitable for the size of bird. The easiest way to fit the gauze is to bend it for support on two sides and lay it in the tray.

Place a perch so that the bird can access food and water easily. In the case of seriously ill birds it is a good idea to place a perch just above the wire mesh floor so that the bird's tail will rest on the mesh

Molting

Birds change their plumage every year. The old worn-out feathers fall out and new ones replace them. This process normally occurs at the end of the summer and takes approximately six weeks. It is a natural process which every bird goes through. They will sometimes be less active, but this will improve once the molt is over. Molting demands a lot of energy. If you make sure that your birds get enough egg food during the molt it will be over quickly and you will have beautiful birds at the end. After the molt, the birds are ready for the next show season.

Young birds molt within a few weeks after they have become independent. They change their adolescent plumage for their adult feathers. They will then get their full color. The dull colors are replaced by the vivid, bright colors of the adult birds.

Prevention

Nursing birds is not easy and prevention is always better, so here are a number of tips.

Hazards in the house

- Make sure that other pets, such as dogs and cats, cannot get near your bird's cage. If you let your bird out of its cage, make sure that the cat is not in the same room and that all the doors are closed.

- In the kitchen your bird is at risk of burning itself on the stove. Don't let your bird fly in the kitchen or cover the stove.

- Birds can seriously harm themselves if they fly at the window at full speed. They don't expect a window to be there. In the most serious case, they can break their neck. In the first few days, only let your bird fly when it is dark. It will then get used to the size of the room and will not fly against the window as quickly in the daylight. There is a far smaller risk when you have drawn the blinds or curtains, of course.

Yellow-crested Cockatoo

- Birds can get stuck between doors that are being opened or closed. A bird walking on the floor is especially at risk. Be careful that you don't tread on your bird if it is walking on the ground.

- Remove poisonous houseplants or at least keep them out of the room where you let your birds fly. When buying new houseplants ask whether they are poisonous for pets.

General preventive measures

- Prevent excessive growth of nails and beaks by providing perches of suitable thickness and plenty of gnawing opportunities (twigs, iodine blocks). If the nails need to be trimmed, use sharp nail scissors. Hold the nail against the light so that you can see where the blood vessels are. Make sure that you don't cut into them. If the foot does start bleeding try to stop it by holding it in cold water, but it is better to singe it closed with a burning cigarette, for example.

• Only feed your birds food which they are meant to have and never let them share your food. Fat, spiced foods and lots of sugar are harmful to their health.

• Don't let your birds catch a cold; make sure that they are not exposed to draughts.

• Prevent vermin in their cages. Use an insecticide before you prepare the cages for the breeding season. Birds can suffer from blood mites, especially young birds in the nest.

• Keep flies and midges out as far as possible by placing fly nets in front of open windows and doors. Mosquitoes can cause pocks in canaries.

• Also check for mice regularly. Try to keep the aviary as mice-free as possible. If you see traces of mice (such as droppings and evidence of gnawing) start fighting them as soon as possible. They turn into a plague faster than you can imagine. Mice cause unrest among birds at night and spread diseases; they soil the floor, smell and cause damage to the aviary.

• You can generally prevent a lot of diseases and suffering by paying good attention to hygiene. Make sure that cages, feed and drink bowls and perches are cleaned regularly. This prevents a lot of problems.

• It is best to contact the vet if you encounter broken wings or legs.

Crimson-rumped Waxbill

There are many different species of birds which can be kept in an aviary very well. There is a bird to suit every taste. As earlier mentioned we restrict ourselves in this book to the most common parrots, parakeets and finches.

Parakeets

Lovebirds

Who does not know them, these cute little African dwarf parrots in their colorful suits. They are not only available in all sorts of bright colors, but also in a range of pastel colors. They measure 5.1 - 6.5 inches and can become twelve years old. They are fertile at nine months old, but because of the risk of egg binding, it is better to wait until they are a year old. They will lay 3 to 7 eggs per nest. If you take

the chicks out of the nest in time – when they are just about to fly out – they will become tame very quickly. Lovebirds do not have great demands regarding caging and, depending on the color, you can buy them in any price category. They are nice birds to have around and they also make good breeding birds.

Australian Parakeets

Australia is rich in forests and over the centuries a multitude of eucalyptus trees developed. Parakeets live and nest in these trees. You can find a lot of pictures on the internet and in books, but at exhibitions you can see them in the flesh. As a beginner, choose one of the species which are easier to keep and to breed. There are a lot of species of Australian Parakeets. We do not have enough space to deal with all of them in this book,

a perfect bird guide

which is why we merely provide an overview here.

Barred Parakeet

Barred Parakeets belong to the family of Thick-mouthed Parakeets: *Bolborhynchus*.

Several species from this genus are quite well known: The Barred Parakeet, the Peruvian Barred Parakeet, the Catherine Parakeet (*B. l. domestica*), the Red-fronted Parakeet, the Andean Parakeet, the Mountain Parakeet, the Roberts' Parakeet, the Margarit's Parakeet, the Red-billed Parakeet and the Gray-hooded Parakeet. They are beautiful birds, which always look at you alertly with their beady eyes. You can keep a single example as a pet bird in your living room, but they are actually birds which really enjoy the company of others of their kind. They are happiest in a bigger group in a spacious aviary.

Budgerigar

This is a parakeet species we all know. We regularly see Budgerigars in blue, green and yellow, with the attractively colored spots on their beaks. More and more color varieties are appearing. A Budgerigar really loves to fly around, which means that it should ideally be kept in an indoor or an outdoor aviary. Bear in mind that you will always find a layer of seeds, sand, feathers and dust around the aviary or cage. If you cannot stand this, then an outdoor aviary is probably the best option. Budgerigars can be kept together with Cockatiels and Bourke's Parakeets. They live in groups, so if you want to keep just one bird in a cage in your living room, you will need to give it enough attention.

Bourke's Parrot

Budgerigar

Rosella

The name Rosella probably derives from Rosehill, a suburb of Sydney where these birds were first spotted. There are many different species of these birds and you will first have to figure out which one exactly you want. As far as caging is concerned, you need to take into account that an outdoor aviary or flight needs to be at least three to

Rosella

four meters long and at least a meter wide. Some species live in groups; others don't, so pay attention to this when deciding on which birds to keep. They can be somewhat aggressive, and don't assume that they will be fine again tomorrow, as it might be too late by then. When putting pairs together, you also need to pay attention to whether the birds get on with each other.

Cockatiels

The Cockatiel is a very popular and much loved cage and aviary bird. It is of a calm and peaceful nature. In the wild, they live in small groups and have a migratory lifestyle. Some birds keep watch while others eat. There is a clear difference between the male and the female bird. Bear in mind that a Cockatiel easily can become 15 years old. The Cockatiel is a gregarious bird which does not like to be alone. If you buy two males or two females, after a while one will start behaving like a cock and the other like a hen, so don't think that you have actually been given a couple. Two birds become attached to each other. A bird kept on its own will become tame more quickly, but you will need to invest a lot of time in it, otherwise it will be very unhappy.

Cockatiel

Parrots

There are more than 300 parrot species. Parrots vary in length from ten centimeters (dwarf parrots) to one meter (macaw).

They also range from having plain plumage to being very colorful, and from being quiet to very mobile and playful. Parrots live a long time. Parakeets and lovebirds can easily become teenagers, and macaws, amazons and cockatoos can reach 60 years or more. Large parrot species include the African parrots, amazons, macaws and cockatoos. The following is a general overview of characteristics, appearance and behavior. But note that exceptions confirm the rule.

Cockatoos

Cockatoos originate in Indonesia, New Guinea and Australia. They vary from 12 inches (Goffin's Cockatoo) to about 22 inches (Salmon-crested Cockatoo and Palm Cockatoo). All cockatoos share one characteristic: their crest. Some species have a crest that is always visible, even when lying flat on the head.
An example is the well known Australian Sulphur-crested Cockatoo. Other cockatoos have a smaller crest, which is not visible when the bird is resting. This is the case with the Goffin's Cockatoo, the Bare-eyed Cockatoo and the Philippine Cockatoo.
When cockatoos are irritated or excited, or when they want to impress others, they raise their crest.

Cockatoos are often regarded as the clowns of the parrot family. As soon as they wake up, they begin to play and they don't stop until they go to sleep. They play with food, toys, twigs, each other or with humans. They are also talented acrobats. They love to hang underneath bars, ropes or twigs and they can perform all sorts of tricks.

Salmon-crested Cockatoo

Screws and locks are not safe from their strong beaks. They observe exactly how you open the doors and, sooner than you think, they can open them as quickly as you shut them. They chew on everything. Therefore always ensure that fresh twigs are available for your parrot. Cockatoos do not differentiate between a cherry twig you have given them and your fine cherry-wood furniture. Therefore, it is important that you always offer them something they are allowed to destroy.

Eclectus Parrot

and good-natured birds, and they need a big flight aviary. If they are housed in too small a space, they will damage their tail feathers on the bars, or pluck out their feathers from boredom.

Blue-and-yellow Macaw

Eclectus Parrots

The various varieties of Eclectus Parrot originate in New Guinea, Indonesia and Cape York in Far-north Queensland. Most species are named after the area where they originate, such as the Halmahera and the Solomon Parrot. The difference between male and female is very obvious with the Eclectus Parrots. The males are mostly green; the females are brilliantly red and blue. Depending on the sub-species, they have various shades or extra colors. Eclectus Parrots can be quiet, kind-natured birds, but they do have a very loud voice. They are not nearly as destructive as cockatoos.

Macaws

Macaws run the show in bird parks and zoos. They are beautifully colored with an impressive beak and an equally impressive screech. They are, however, normally quiet

There are small dwarf macaws as well as the better-known, larger macaws. The bigger species can reach a length of one meter, including the tail. Today, more macaws are bred in captivity, and there are plenty of offspring available. There are currently no legal imports to Australia. Some macaw species are critically endangered. This is the case with the Hyacinth Macaw, Lear's Macaw and Spix's Macaw. Only approximately 40 Spix's Macaws are known to exist in captivity. Only one individual, a male, lives in Brazil in the wild. An international rescue project has been started for this species, where every possible effort is made to prevent the Spix's Macaw from becoming extinct in the wild.

Amazons

As the name indicates, amazons originate in South America. They are spread over a large area, which includes large parts of South and Central America. Some sub-species, however, have only a very small area of distribution. This is due to natural barriers, nesting opportunities and the availability of food. All the Amazon species, and there are approximately 27 of them, are basically green. Besides green, they have other colors, which depend on the sub-species. The Yellow-faced Amazon and the Greater Yellow-faced Amazon have a lot of yellow on their head. Other colors common with amazons are orange, red, blue, purple and white, in all sorts of nuances and combinations.

The sizes of amazons range from just under 30 centimeters (Cuban Amazon and White-fronted Amazon) to about 45 centimeters (such as the rare Imperial Amazon). This depends on the species, the sex and the area of origin. Males are often a little more strongly built than females, but exceptions prove the rule here, too.

Many amazons become good talkers or imitators of all sorts of sounds, depending on the species

Red-browed Amazon

and the individual. The Blue-fronted Amazon and the Yellow-fronted Amazon are usually good talkers, but success is not guaranteed. To teach a bird to talk, whistle or sing you must devote hours to the task every day. However, this is not a guarantee that your bird will say whatever you want it to. Often they find screeching doors, phones ringing, door bells and barking dogs far more interesting. Or they stick to typical bird sounds.

The Pionus varieties or Red-tailed Parrots also come from South America. These are pretty, friendly cage and aviary birds as long as they feel at home. Most Pionus

Grey Parrot

varieties are not too large, but their ability to talk is limited.

African parrots

These include the Timneh Grey Parrot, the Meyer's Parrot, the Senegal Parrot and the Congo Grey Parrot. The Grey Parrot is often found in living rooms, where it is a sociable and valued member of the family. It is famous for its ability to imitate, but again, this is not guaranteed. It is an easy bird to breed, which means that there are plenty of offspring on offer. Grey Parrots born in captivity are usually very affectionate, playful, eager to learn and quiet, although there are some notorious screamers among them. Grey Parrots are very susceptible to stress, which is often expressed in plucking their own plumage. This can also be a sign of boredom.

Finches

Canaries

The canary is one of the most popular cage birds. It is a very popular pet bird because of its song.

Canaries are generally divided into three groups:
• Song canaries
• Color canaries
• Type canaries

The song canary is obviously kept for its song. There are three species of song canaries, which are the Harzer, the Waterslager and the Timbrado. To a layman the songs of the different types might seem the same, but to a song breeder the songs of the color canaries sound more like screams. Song canaries are specifically selected for their song quality and each species has its own song ('tour' in the breeders-jargon). Only the male birds sing.

Color canaries are often kept as pet birds in the living room, but they are even more often kept as aviary birds. The canary is quite suitable for beginners, as it doesn't demand a lot in terms of care and breeds quite easily. Show breeders almost always breed them in breeding cages and often use one male for several females. You can also breed them in an aviary. This works best if you place twice as many females in the aviary as males. You can buy special nesting bowls (Harzer bowls) in pet shops, but a nesting box made of bars is also

Canary

the nest. The parents want to start with a new nest and use the chicks' feathers as nesting material. If this happens, you can put the young into a special baby cage which is hung onto the breeding cage. The parents cannot reach the chicks then, but they can still feed them through the bars. When there are young you should feed extra egg food. It is also advisable to feed extra germinated seeds and some green food.

Color canaries are bred in almost all colors. Although most people think that canaries should be yellow, the original color is green with black stripes. The red canary developed from crossing in the Black-hooded Red Siskin. Color canaries are divided into several groups:
Pigmented, which are just as the wild form.

suitable for canaries. Sisal rope is good nesting material for canaries. A canary lays approximately four to six blue-green speckled eggs. When a canary has laid an egg, you remove it and replace it by an artificial egg. After the third egg has been laid you put the real egg back. Then all the eggs hatch at the same time. If you don't do that there might be three days age difference between the first born and the last born chick, because the female starts brooding from the first egg. The last chicks often stay behind in the nest and also die quicker.

Young canaries are independent when the V-shape appears in the tail, which is approximately after six weeks. It can happen that the parents pluck the young. This usually happens after they have left

Canary

Lipochromes, here the pigment has disappeared and the yellow, red or white (secondary) color remains. Mosaics, i.e. birds with a standardized marking on the breast, wings and head.

The type canaries are specifically selected on the basis of format, model, posture and/or plumage. The following species are being bred:
Frilled species, here the plumage structure has changed. The feathers are often longer and often curl in various places.
Posture species. They need to hold themselves in a certain stance and stand tall on their legs.
Form species. They are bred specifically to fit into a certain form/ model. They are often quite big around the chest area.
Crested species. They display a crest on their head.
Marked species. The most popular one of these is the lizard canary with its scaly marking and an unmarked head.

As you can see, there is enough choice if you want to start with canaries.

Zebra Finches

The zebra finch (*Taeniopygia guttata*) is probably the most popular aviary bird of them all. It belongs in the waxbill category. Almost anyone who keeps birds or ever kept birds has had these chirpy Australian birds in his aviary at some point. More than a hundred color variations have been bred

Zebra Finch

from zebra finches. The original color is grey and this wild color is still very popular.

In the wild this bird lives a nomadic life and moves through all of Australia. You can always find it near watering places.
They live in large groups and brood in colonies. Their food in the wild consists of all sorts of grass seeds and some insects. As aviary birds, they thrive on a basic mix of tropical seeds and some egg food, grit and some green food once in a while. In the wild zebra finches breed shortly after the rainy period, as this is when there is the largest supply of fresh grass seeds. As aviary birds they also like high humidity. You can ensure this by offering them bathing water several times a week, which they will definitely love.

Breeders who breed zebra finches for shows almost always do this in breeding cages of at least 16 x 16 x 16 inches. They also breed well if you have several pairs in an aviary together. They will definitely start incubating then. Zebra finches are quite brutal and dominant towards other birds. If a zebra finch feels like it, it might even occupy the nest of another bird, even if there are already eggs in there. They will also be the first on the feed bowl to pick out the tastiest seeds. This makes them less attractive for some breeders and it is a reason why many switch over to other birds.

Zebra finches are not picky concerning their nesting box and their nesting material. They'll take anything they can get.

It is easy to see the difference between the sexes: the males have an orange-brown spot on the cheek, black chest markings, chestnut flanks and the beak is also a little redder. The females miss these markings.

Society Finch

Society Finches (*Lonchura domestica*) don't exist in the wild. They have been created in Japan as hybrids of different types of Manias. Society Finches have often been used as foster parents for different species of waxbills. I once saw five different species of chicks in the nest of Society Finches, all of which were raised without any problems. Luckily, there has been a trend towards letting waxbills brood naturally, but if there hadn't been

Society Finches before there certainly wouldn't be as many waxbills for sale, or only at very high prices.

In the sixties, the usually pied Society Finches were selected towards single-colored birds, partly by hybridization with Black-headed Munias. This means that these birds have become worthy of being

Society Finch

shown. There are also different types of mutations, besides the original mocha-brown there are also red-brown, grey, pastel, faded-wing, ino, crested and frilled. From the pieds, birds have been selected according to their color patterns. Some specialist breeding clubs have made the Society Finch popular as an exhibition bird.

Society Finches breed easily. They prefer half-open nesting boxes. You can offer them grass or coconut fiber as nesting material and some sisal rope to finish off the nest.

They can be kept together with other species without too many problems. Breeding might be difficult in an aviary; however, as they will all try to get into one nesting box to sleep. They are easily pushed aside by other birds in the aviary. This is why they are usually bred in breeding cages, which should have the same measurements as those for zebra finches. They also eat the same food as zebra finches.

Gouldian Finch

If you see a Gouldian Finch (*Erythrura gouldiae*) for the first time you will think it was painted.

Gouldian Finch

This vividly colored bird with all its distinctive colors is a real gem in any aviary. The Gouldian Finch originates in northern Australia. There are three species in the wild: the black-head, the red-head and the less common orange-head, which is often called yellow-head. The Gouldian Finch is heavily

protected in the wild; the whole population is estimated to be no more than 1,500 birds in the wild. A number of breeding programmers have been started to ensure the survival of these birds in the wild.

Luckily there is larger supply of Gouldian Finches as aviary birds and they are being bred all over the world. In the sixties, after the export ban from Australia, they were too popular with dealers and natural selection for quality was out of the focus.

All the eggs were put under Society Finches and the Gouldian Finch even forgot how to brood. Even today, Gouldian Finches have the reputation of being very weak birds which need to be kept at a minimum temperature of 86 ºF during the day and at 41 ºF at night!

If you intend to keep these birds in an outdoor aviary, you should buy your birds from a breeder where they were already kept outdoors. It is best to buy them in the summer or in early autumn so that they can easily adapt to the colder nights. In the winter they need access to a frost-free shelter at night.

It is very easy to tell males and females apart. The female has duller colors but the same markings as the male. Gouldian Finches can easily be kept in a communal aviary, even with several other pairs. Make sure that there are always excess nesting boxes. A special nesting box has been developed for Gouldian Finches which you can buy in pet shops. It is a closed nesting box with a round entrance hole and a small landing on the front where the male often sits to hold watch. These birds always mate in the nesting box, which means that it has to be more spacious than nesting boxes for other species. They will also start brooding in a slightly larger breeding cage.

Gouldian Finches have a strong preference for dark nesting material (hay, coconut fiber). In the wild they usually brood in splits or holes of trees. It is darker in these spots, so the chicks cannot be spotted as easily. Nature has found a solution here: Gouldian Finches are born with luminous papillae around the beak, so the parents know exactly where to put the food. When these papillae dry up after the young have left the nest, they are independent. When the Gouldian Finch becomes fertile, the male's beak color becomes almost white with a red or yellow spot and the hen's beak becomes almost completely lead-grey.

Young Gouldian Finches have not yet got their parents' bright colors, as they would then be easy prey for their natural enemies. Young birds are very sensitive to changes in their environment. After you have separated them from their parents you should place them in a flight from which they shouldn't really be moved again. The move to another cage can even cause the chicks to stop molting and to remain in half

Gouldian Finch

their adolescent coat for a full year, even if the new cage is exactly the same as the old.

These birds should be fed on a good exotic mix supplemented with Japanese millet (which they love), millet spray, egg food, grit and some minerals.

If you want to let your birds bring up their chicks themselves, then you also need to add some pinkies and buffalo worms to their daily menu, as these contain vital proteins. Some mutations have occurred in Gouldian Finches, such as the white-chested, pastel, dilute, yellow, blue and cinnamon (brown).

Gouldian Finches are very sensitive to airway mites. These mites live in the birds' throats and stomachs and they irritate the birds very badly. Birds often sneeze when they are infected. If you don't do anything about it, it will get worse very quickly. Your birds can even die of it. The mite can be passed on to other birds too. You can easily treat your birds against airway mites by putting one or two drops against ear mites into their neck. It will usually offer relief within a day. Keep on observing your birds closely, as the mites' eggs can hatch after a week and everything may start again.

Shafttail

Shafttail

The Shafttail (*Poephila acuticauda*) originates from Northern Australia. There are two different species, i.e. the red-beaked and the yellow-beaked. Orange-beaked birds occur in the transitional region, and it is not a separate species but a transitional form. You can easily recognize the Shafttail by its tail feathers, which are very long in comparison to its close relative, the Black-throated Finch (*Poephila cincta*). The Black-throated Finch has a black bib and the same breech-markings, but it also has a black beak and no long tail feathers. The Masked Finch has

only a small bib and a mask around its beak. The beak is yellow and the length of the tail feathers is between that of the Shafttail and that of the Black-throated Finch. It is very difficult to see a difference between the male and the female Shafttail. In the case of the male, the color on the head is a light grey and the bib and breech-marking is a little bigger; in the case of the red-beaked species, the beak is also often a deeper red. As far as feeding and care are concerned, the Shafttail has similar demands as the Gouldian Finch, although it is not necessary to feed extra Japanese millet.

Shafttails can be kept well both in communal aviaries and in breeding cages. They can be quite dominant, although they are not normally too aggressive towards other birds. However, there might be problems in the breeding season if you keep several Shafttails together, or if you keep them together with Black-throated Finches.
If they don't fight for their own territory there is a big chance that the young are hybrids between these two species. Shafttails breed both in closed and in semi-open nesting boxes. Hay, coconut fiber and sisal rope are all accepted as nesting material. The following mutations are known in Shafttails: brown, Isabel, ino, grey and pastel.

Diamond Firetail

The Diamond Firetail (*Stagonopleura guttata*) originates in South-Eastern Australia and is a more sturdily built bird. Its call is also easy to recognize. There is hardly any difference between the male and the hen, but the hen is a little more lead-grey on the head. Diamond Firetails need to have plenty of flying space, as they become fat very quickly.

Diamond Firetail

They can be kept in a brooding cage but the measurements need to be bigger than those for other waxbills. The minimum size is 80 x 40 x 40 cm. It is better if they are kept in flights, simply because they become fat very quickly. In a communal aviary the Diamond Firetail can be very dominant towards other birds of a similar or smaller build. They can, however, quite easily be kept with other European species and neophemas (a parakeet-species), for example. The care and breeding are similar to those of the Shafttail. The following mutations are known of the Diamond Firetail: yellow-beaked, brown, Isabel, dilute and opaline.

Star Finch

The Star Finch (*Neochmia ruficauda*) originates in Western, Northern and Eastern Australia. The nominate form has an almost white belly and the sub-species (*N. clarescens*), which is kept by breeders, has a yellow belly. It is easy to tell males and females apart. The male's red mask is a lot bigger and the yellow on its belly is also a lot more intensive.

Star Finch

These birds can easily be kept in communal aviaries, and they can also be kept outdoors in winter as long as they have access to a frost-free night shelter. They also breed easily in breeding cages. Care and breeding are similar to those of the Shafttail. When the female is ready for brooding she often gets a black stripe on her beak. The following mutations are known of the Star Finch: yellow-beaked, pastel and pied.

Red-headed Parrot Finch

Red-headed Parrot Finch

Parrot Finches (*Erythrura psittacea*) are primarily green birds, often with red and blue markings. The different species are found in a wide distribution area, from Malaysia to New Guinea and Australia.

There are ten different species with a number of sub-species, of which the red-headed and the tricoloured Parrot Finches (*Erythura trichroa*) are the best known. They are very lively birds which are always active. In an aviary with plants they will be less obvious because of their green plumage, but you will still get to see them a lot because they are active flyers. There is hardly any difference between hen and male, the male has a slightly deeper red on the head and often has a few red feathers in the anal region.

Red-headed Parrot Finches are very suitable for communal aviaries, but they need to have a frost-free shelter available in the winter. They breed in all sorts of nesting boxes or even build their own nest in shrubs or behind conifer twigs and they make a sort of tunnel as an entrance. The nesting material in the aviary consists of grass and coconut fiber.

The following mutations have developed: sea-green, pied, yellow black-eyed and lutino.

The care is almost identical to that of the Shafttails. They love bathing and they should have clean bathing water available every day.

Java Sparrow

The Java Sparrow or Java Finch (*Padda oryzivora*) was one of the first waxbills to be imported at the end of the eighteenth century. They originate in South-Eastern Asia, where they can be a real pest for the farmers by raiding rice fields. They have been bred a lot as songbirds and have become popular show birds through their always tight plumage. They can be bred both in an aviary and in breeding

Java Sparrow

cages. They can also be kept together with several pairs.

You need to keep a close eye on these birds. It is quite common to have a more aggressive individual in the aviary, which raids the nests of the other birds. It can sometimes go well for a few years until you suddenly have a trouble-maker in your aviary. They usually brood in closed nesting boxes and the nesting material consists of grass or hay and coconut fiber. Java Sparrows lay up to six to nine eggs which hatch 21 days after the first egg has been laid, as long as they have been fertilized.

It is difficult to tell the sexes apart, but the males have a slightly bigger beak. The underside of the V-form of the beak is sharper on males. On females the underside is rounder. The eye-ring is also of a deeper red in the case of the male, especially in the breeding period.

Besides the wild color, the white Java Sparrow is also very popular. This white form has been selected from the pied. To keep the format and the plumage of the white variety at a high standard, they are usually crossed pied x white and vice versa. These crossings also bring forth pied chicks, which you can distinguish from the white chicks straight after birth. The pied ones have a black spot on the beak whereas the white birds have a white beak. The following mutations have occurred in Java Sparrows: besides the pied and the white birds, there are also isabels, pastels and opalines.

Java Sparrows are winter-hardy, which means that they can be kept outdoors all year round as long as they have been outdoors from the summer. The feeding consists of a tropical or budgerigar seed mix, which should be complemented by paddy (unpeeled rice), egg food, grit, germinated seeds and some green food. Java Sparrows love to bathe, which is why you should regularly offer them fresh bathing water.

White-headed Munia

White-headed Munia

Munias belong to the large genus of lonchuras, to which Munias, Yellow-rumped Mannikin and Society Finches also belong. The White-headed Munia (*Lonchura maja*) exists in Southern Thailand, Malaysia, Sumatra, Java and Bali. There is hardly any visible difference between males and hens. Birds with a whiter head are often males; the females are often

Green Singer

Shafttails and their behavior and breeding is the same as that of the Java Sparrow. Munias often suffer from long nails, which you thus need to check regularly. Cut the nails to just before the quick, which you can see if you hold the nail to the light.

The advantages and disadvantages of the White-headed Munia are the same as those of the Java Sparrow.

You can find more information about White-headed Munias and other lonchuras in our description of the Society Finch.

Green Singer

The Green Singer (*Serinus mozambicus*) is one of the best known African finch species. Its great song in particular has made it very popular.
The Green Singer has eleven subspecies which live all over Africa. The Green Singer belongs to the Cinis, just as the canary.
Male and female can easily be distinguished, as the female has a marking on the chest which looks like a necklace, and it is a little duller in color. In some of the subspecies the female is completely yellow on the chest. You can breed Green Singers both in breeding cages and in aviaries. You need to be aware, however, that they can be very aggressive towards other aviary inhabitants, especially if they belong to smaller species, such as the White-rumped Seedeater and other species of the same color.

darker in color. This is not always the case, however. The color of the head varies depends on the region where the birds come from.

When you buy White-headed Munias in a shop it is best to buy a number of them and to give them all differently colored foot rings. You can then keep a close eye on which birds form pairs with each other. If you buy your birds from a breeder who knows his birds, he can tell you the differences between males and females and you will be sure that you are really buying a pair.

As far as care is concerned, they have the same demands as the

a perfect bird guide

If you want to breed Green Singers in a communal aviary, then it is best to keep them together with slightly bigger species, as these can defend themselves better. The most popular nesting boxes are the semi-open box and the grid nesting box. Grass stalks and coconut fiber are used as nesting material and the nest is finished off with sisal rope and feathers. Young Green Singers look like the hen. Green Singers are also often used to breed hybrids with canaries. Especially the males from these crossings can sing very well. There seems to be a blue mutation of the Green Singer, but very little is known about this.

Their food consists of a good tropical mix supplemented with canary seeds, weed seeds and egg food. Grit must also not be missing. In the breeding period the diet should be supplemented with germinated seeds, green food and some live food. Although they can cope well with the cold, it is better to keep them in a frost-free environment in the winter.

Weavers

Weavers owe their name to the way they build their nests. Whilst hanging from twigs and canes they weave sometimes enormous hanging nests. There are more than 270 weaver species, most of which live in Africa and Asia. Most weaver species are colony birds and they live in groups of sometimes thousands of birds. Weavers are also polygamous, which means that a male often has several females, sometimes up to six.

Just as in the case of the whydahs, most weaver males have a nuptial plumage and a resting plumage. In the resting plumage there is hardly any difference between Males and females. They are very popular aviary birds because they weave interesting nests on twigs and mesh and because of their beautiful colors. The most commonly kept species belong to the following groups: Black Bishop (orange, grenadier, flames, black-bellied), the Village Weaver (small, large, egg-yellow) and the Red-billed Quelea.

Weavers are strong birds which can be kept in an outdoor aviary all year round. They can become very

Zanzibar Bishop

Cuba Finch

old. There are weavers which have lived in their aviary for a good fifteen years and whose age was not known when they were bought. Unfortunately they also have a bad habit: they like to raid the nests of other aviary inhabitants to use the nesting material themselves. It is thus advisable to keep them with bigger species if you want to breed. You need to be aware, however, that breeding successes with weavers are exceptions, but maybe this is exactly the challenge you are looking for? If you have an aviary and you don't necessarily want to breed, then weavers definitely shouldn't be missing.

As far as care is concerned, they don't have any special requirements. They'll eat almost anything you offer them. As a basic food you can feed them a tropical mix, canary seed, weed seeds, egg food, germinated seeds, green food and some mealworms.

Cuba Finch

Cuba finches (*Tiaris canora*) aren't only found on Cuba, but also in the whole of Central America and also in the northern regions of South America. There are five species of Cuba finches with several sub-species. The Cuba finch is the best known, followed by the Yellow-faced Grassquit (*Tiaris olivacea*) and the black-chested Cuba Finch (*Tiaris bicolor*). The males are more noticeable in terms of colors and markings, the females have very light markings and duller colors.

You can achieve good breeding results with Cuba finches, both in breeding cages and in an aviary. They look best in an aviary. Cuba finches can easily be kept in a communal aviary, although they will enter the nests of other aviary inhabitants once in a while! It is inadvisable to keep several (species of) Cuba finches in the same space during the breeding season, as the males will chase each other until there are casualties. They can be kept together in the resting period. Especially when birds have only recently been placed together, you need to keep an eye on them to make sure that peace is ensured.

The nesting material consists of grass stalks and coconut fiber. They prefer shrubs and small trees as nesting locations where they can build the nests themselves. If this is not possible a semi-open nesting box will also do. They make an entrance hole at the side of the nest. The three to four eggs are light green/ bluish and have red stripes. Both parents sit on the eggs. Incubation takes approximately twelve to fourteen days and the young leave the nest after approximately four weeks. The parents will often start with a new batch straight away. It is then advisable to remove the young from the aviary when they are approximately six weeks old, as there is a chance that the male will chase the young because he sees them as rivals.

The care is similar to that of the Shafttails. Especially during the breeding period it is advisable to enrich the general food with some live food. In the winter it is best to keep them frost-free at a temperature of at least 50 °F. Cuba finches are reasonable singers.

American Finches
The group of American finches has never become as popular as the finch species of Africa, Asia, Australia and Europe, despite the beautiful colors of the males. But why? Imported birds are regularly offered for sale. The purchase price varies a lot from very cheap to very expensive. Breeding successes are achieved regularly. The problem is that it is often quite difficult to get females, and the females of the different species also look very much alike. American finches exist in South, Central and North America. The best known species are: the Indigo Bunting (*Passerina cyanea*) which is deep blue, the Varied Bunting (*Passerina versicolor*), the Painted Bunting (*Passerina ciris*), the Orange-breasted Bunting (*Passerina leclancherii*) and the Lazuli Bunting (*Passerina amoena*).

Other American seed-eaters are: the Blue-black Grassquit (*Volatinia jacarina*), the Ultra-marine Grosbeak, which belongs to the

Orange-breasted Bunting

Northern Cardinal

Some finches have nuptial and resting plumage, just as weavers. In its resting plumage the male looks just like the female. It is obvious that you should offer your birds fresh drinking and bathing water on a daily basis.

American finches can easily be kept in a communal aviary, although they can be quite dominant in the breeding season, especially the Ultra-marine Grosbeak. If you want to breed it is best to keep them in pairs, just as European songbirds. The species from South and Central America should be kept at a minimum temperature of 50 °F in the winter months. Although the Painted Bunting would obviously prefer to be outdoors day and night all year round, as the North American species are winter-hardy.

Their song is beautiful, although some species hardly ever sing. The Ultra-marine Grosbeak will only sing when its young are leaving the nest and the Painted Bunting only sings in the middle of the night.

genus Cyanocompsa and has six subspecies. The male is primarily cobalt to violet-blue and the female is almost completely brown.

As far as their food is concerned they don't have too many demands: a mix of tropical or canary seeds enriched with weed seeds (fresh, although semi-ripe is better), grit, egg food, germinated seeds and green food. It is vital to offer them live food such as buffalo worms and pinkies in the breeding season. It is also important to feed them weed seeds. These contain a lot of carotene, which they need to keep a beautiful color.

Cardinals
There are twelve different species of cardinals, most of which live in South American, although they can also be found in Central and North America. Although one of its names, 'Pigmy Cardinal' would have you believe that it belongs to the Cardinal family, the Black-crested Finch (*Lophospingus pusillus*) belongs to a different genus. This genus is also noticeably smaller than the real cardinals, which

are approximately the size of black-birds. Some species have a crest whereas others have a smooth head.

The best-known species is the Yellow Cardinal (*Gubernatrix cristata*), which is primarily green in color with yellow on the head, a black bib and crest. The female has only very little yellow on the head and is more whitish in color.

The Northern Cardinal (*Cardinalis cardinalis*) lives in North America and the body of the male is completely red including the crest and it has a red mask around the beak. The female is yellow-brown in color and the mask is quite vague, but the beak is bright red. The Red-crested Cardinal (*Paroaria coronata*) is very distinct with its red head, crest and chest, its white lower body and its grey back and mantle. There is hardly any difference between the sexes in this species. The female is often a little smaller and its red is also less vivid.

Cardinals can easily be kept in a communal aviary with other birds of a similar size, such as weavers, thrushes and starling species.

They can disturb the rest of smaller bird species, especially during the breeding period. They are best kept in an aviary with plants, and they also breed best here. They build their nest in shrubs, conifers or in nesting baskets. As nesting material, they use twigs, grass stems, coconut fiber and hair.

Their feeding consists of a coarse seed mix (the ones for lovebirds or neophemas are ideal) enriched with paddy, oats, millet spray, safflower seeds, egg food and grit. During the breeding period they need to be given extra egg food, germinated seeds, green food, general food and live food, such as mealworms, maggots and ant eggs. They also need fresh drinking and bathing water on a regular basis. Cardinals are winter-hardy but it is better to offer them a night shelter where they can seek protection.

Northern Cardinal

www.birdsnways.com
The complete guide to pet birds, pet parrots and exotic birds

www.avianbreeder.com
The premier site for breeders and buyers of exotic birds

www.toohaven.org
An avian rescue center for all species of cockatoos.

Red-fronted Macaw

a perfect bird guide